ORIENTAL ANTIQUES

COMPILED BY TONY CURTIS

While every care has been taken in the compiling of information contained in this volume the publishers cannot accept any liability for loss, financial or otherwise, incurred by reliance placed on the information herein.

All prices quoted in this book are obtained from a variety of auctions in various countries and are converted to dollars at the rate of exchange prevalent at the time of sale.

ISBN 0-86248-022-1

Copyright © Lyle Publications MCMLXXXII
Published by Lyle Publications, Glenmayne, Galashiels, Selkirkshire, Scotland.

INTRODUCTION

This book is one of a series specially devised to aid the busy professional dealer in his everyday trading. It will also prove to be of great value to all collectors and those with goods to sell, for it is crammed with illustrations, brief descriptions and valuations of hundreds of antiques.

Every effort has been made to ensure that each specialised volume contains the widest possible variety of goods in its particular category though the greatest emphasis is placed on the middle bracket of trade goods rather than on those once-in-a-lifetime museum pieces whose values are of academic rather than practical interest to the vast majority of dealers and collectors.

This policy has been followed as a direct consequence of requests from dealers who sensibly realise that, no matter how comprehensive their knowledge, there is always a need for reliable, up-to-date reference works for identification and valuation purposes.

When using your Antiques and their Values Book to assess the worth of goods, please bear in mind that it would be impossible to place upon any item a precise value which would hold good under all circumstances. No antique has an exactly calculable value; its price is always the result of a compromise reached between buyer and seller, and questions of condition, local demand and the business acumen of the parties involved in a sale are all factors which affect the assessment of an object's 'worth' in terms of hard cash.

In the final analysis, however, such factors cancel out when large numbers of sales are taken into account by an experienced valuer, and it is possible to arrive at a surprisingly accurate assessment of current values of antiques; an assessment which may be taken confidently to be a fair indication of the worth of an object and which provides a reliable basis for negotiation.

Throughout this book, objects are grouped under category headings and, to expedite reference, they progress in price order within their own categories. Where the description states 'one of a pair' the value given is that for the pair sold as such.

The publishers wish to express their sincere thanks
to the following for their kind help and assistance
in the production of this volume:

JANICE MONCRIEFF
NICOLA PARK
CARMEN MILIVOYEVICH
ELAINE HARLAND
MAY MUTCH
MARGOT RUTHERFORD
JENNIFER KNOX
SHONA BROWN
KAREN KILGOUR

Printed by Apollo Press, Worthing, Sussex, England.
Bound by R. J. Acford, Chichester, Sussex, England.

CONTENTS

ARMOUR

Scarce 18th or 19th century Japanese russet face-guard mempo in red and black lacquer. $235 £100

Late 18th century russet iron yukinoshita-do of five main plates, signed Miochin Ki Munemasu.
$750 £320

An Indo-Persian suit of chain mail, 16th/17th century.
$900 £400

A Japanese half suit of armour bearing a gilt monogram. $1,300 £600

A Japanese half suit of armour with fluted Kabuto, four neck lames and eight plate lames.
$1,450 £650

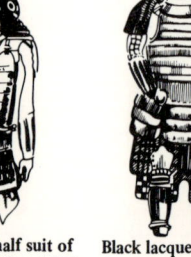

Black lacquered Kon-Ito-Sugake odoshi yokohagi-do of the Edo period, with Hineno style san-mai-bachi.
$1,640 £700

A composite suit of Japanese armour, eight plate Kabuto of lacquered rivetted iron.
$1,500 £700

A complete suit of Japanese armour with black lacquered laced body plates. $1,750 £800

Interesting Kawazutsumi-Hotoke-do, signed Boshu Iwakuni Haruta Masatoki, Edo period. $2,340 £1,000

8

ARMOUR

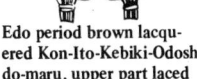

18th century O-Boshi hoshi no kabuto with twenty-four-plate russet iron hachi, signed Masuda Myochin no Kami Ki Munemasa.
$4,680 £2,000

Edo period brown lacquered Kon-Ito-Kebiki-Odoshi do-maru, upper part laced in yellow, orange and green.
$2,455 £1,050

Kabuto with fine russet iron hoshi-bachi of tenkokuzan, signed Nagamichi, mid Edo period. $3,510 £1,500

Asagi-Ito-Odoshi yoko-hagi okegawa-do, signed Myochin Muneysahi saku, 19th century. $4,680 £2,000

19th century Japanese suit of armour.
$5,000 £2,300

Mid Edo period Moegi-Ito-Odoshi dangaie-do, kabuto with black and brown lacquered Hineno style san-mai-bachi, unsigned.
$5,615 £2,400

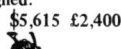

A complete suit of Japanese armour, circa 1750.
$5,250 £2,400

Fine Aka-Shiro-Ito-Odoshi Nimai-do-gusoku, hachi 17th century, mounting 19th century. $8,190 £3,500

Japanese suit of armour bearing the badge of The Daimyo of Kokura.
$35,000 £16,000

9

BRONZE

Chinese bronze circular bowl with inlaid cloisonne banding, 7in. diam. $115 £50

A 19th century Chinese bronze rectangular vessel, with tapering sides cast with panels of Chinese fret and dragon masks, 7½in. long. $125 £55

Japanese bronze oblong box with bird head handles, 9½in. wide. $125 £55

Japanese bronze circular bowl with large rim, 8¾in. $125 £55

Pair of embossed bronze candlesticks entwined with dragons. $150 £65

Japanese bronze circular jardiniere with birds and flowers in bas relief, 40cm. diam. $370 £160

Large Murakami bronze jardiniere, circa 1900, 14½in. high. $450 £200

Late 19th century bronze dish inlaid in gold, silver and bronze, 12in. diam. $620 £275

Late 19th century cast bronze jardiniere, 14in. high. $640 £285

Late 19th century
bronze jardiniere,
16in. high.
        $745 £330

One of a pair of
Thai bronze drums,
48cm. high.
        $2,250 £1,000

Chinese openwork
bronze disc of the
6th/5th century
B.C., 2¼in. diam.
        $5,000 £2,250

Shang dynasty
archaic bronze
wine vessel.
        $5,625 £2,500

10th century Javanese
bronze bowl, 20.9cm.
high. $21,375 £9,500

One of a pair of bronze
cheek-pieces from a
horse's bit, Iranian,
14cm. square.
        $25,875 £11,500

A finely cast archaic
bronze cauldron of
the Shang dynasty,
9¼in. high.
        $45,000 £20,000

Japanese bronze bell
of the Yayoi period,
62cm. high.
        $112,500 £50,000

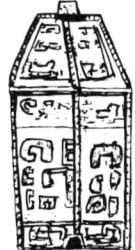

A Shang dynasty bro-
nze Fang I vessel.
        $450,000 £200,000

11

BRONZE ANIMALS

A mid 19th century Japanese, articulated bronze grasshopper. $150 £65

A bronze group of a cat and frog on circular base, unsigned, 8in. high, 6in. diam. $150 £65

Japanese bronze lion. $360 £160

Late 19th century Seiya bronze of an elephant, Japanese, 14in. long. $485 £215

Cambodian gilded bronze antelope, reclining, circa 1880. $600 £265

A large 19th century bronze group of Jan-esha, seated on the back of a three-headed elephant. $755 £335

Bronze fish eagle with Shakudo beak and crystal eyes, signed Mitani, 42.5cm. high. $1,150 £525

Bronze lion cast in the Tang style, 10in. long. $1,195 £530

Japanese bronze eagle on tree trunk with snake at base. $1,350 £600

12

A large 19th century Chinese bronze crane, 7ft. high. $1,575 £700

Late 19th century bronze monkey, marked Hosendo, 6¼in. high. $1,685 £750

One of a pair of early Chinese dogs of Fo. $1,745 £775

One of a pair of Gyoko bronze mandarin ducks, late 19th century, 8¾in. high. $1,845 £850

Late 19th century bronze elephant attacked by tigers, 39cm. long. $3,000 £1,350

Large Japanese bronze model of a tiger, 6ft. 6in. long. $6,750 £3,000

Chinese gilt bronze of the Hau dynasty, depicting a bear seated on its haunches, 9.8cm. high. $47,250 £21,000

Gilt bronze sea dragon from the period of the six dynasties, 5½in. $225,000 £100,000

Tang gilt bronze figure of a striding lion, 6½in. high. $303,750 £135,000

BRONZE FIGURES

Chinese bronze group of a figure and a cow, 8½in. wide. $150 £65

19th century Nepalese bronze Buddha, 8in. high. $225 £100

19th century Chinese bronze of an old man seated on a large fish supported by stylised waves, 8½in. high. $170 £75

19th century Burmese gilt bronze Buddha, 17in. high. $305 £135

Japanese bronze standing figure of a warrior in a fighting pose, 18in. high. $360 £160

Early 19th century Kashmiri style figure of Buddha, 15in. high. $360 £160

A heavy 18th century Chinese bronze Buddha, 10in. high, with traces of gilt. $385 £175

A bronze deity seated playing a Koto, 11¾in. high, late 19th century. $520 £230

Tibetan gilt bronze of a Lama seated on a carpeted podium, 6½in. tall. $655 £290

14

6th/8th century gilt
bronze house shrine,
6½in. high.
$915 £405

16th century Tibetan
bronze of Sherab
Seng-Ge, 7¼in. high.
$1,270 £565

18th century Nep-
alese bronze of
Hayagrava in Yab-
Yum, 6¼in. high.
$1,350 £600

One of a pair of Thai
bronze kneeling figures,
19th century, 79cm.
high. $1,520 £675

Japanese bronze
figure of a man.
$1,520 £675

19th century bronze
figure of an old man,
9in. long.
$1,540 £685

Late Ming dynasty
bronze figure, 11¾in.
high. $1,575 £700

Tibetan bronze of
an abbot, circa 1800,
6¼in. $1,645 £730

Bronze Thai Buddha,
30in. high.
$1,645 £730

BRONZE FIGURES

A large 19th century Japanese bronze group. $1,825 £810

19th century Japanese bronze figure of a Samurai warrior, 10in. high. $2,025 £900

Early 15th century Ming bronze figure of Golden Boy, 6.5in. high. $2,025 £900

17th century Nepalese bronze of the Bodhisattva Avalokitesvara, 5½in. high. $2,250 £1,000

Early 18th century gilt bronze seated figure of Guanyin, 9½in. high. $2,250 £1,000

18th century Nepalese copper and silver figure of Vajravarshi, 6¼in. high. $2,815 £1,250

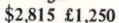

Tibetan bronze of Maitreya seated in Virasana with hands in dharmacakra, circa 1600, 5in. $2,925 £1,300

Japanese red bronze box, signed Yoshiaki, 10.8cm. $3,040 £1,350

13th century pagan figure of the Buddha in bronze, 10¾in. high. $3,375 £1,500

West Tibetan bronze
figure of Kubera wear-
ing jewellery, inlaid
with silver and stones,
8½in. high.
$5,625 £2,500

15th century bronze
bust of the Buddha by
Sukh'o'tai, 28½in.
high. $6,750 £3,000

A rare Samaskanda
group, Indian, 11th/
13th century.
$11,250 £5,000

Nepalese gilt bronze
figure of Maitreya,
25½in. high.
$12,150 £5,400

14th century Chinese
gilt bronze figure of
Guatama, 20cm. high.
$22,500 £10,000

An 18th century Sino-
Tibetan gilt bronze of
the Hdarmapala Yaman-
taka in the form of
Vajrabhairava, 57.1cm.
high. $39,375 £17,500

A 14th century Nepal-
ese gilt copper figure
of Guatama seated in
dhyanasana, 58.8cm.
high. $78,750 £35,000

11th century Chola
bronze figure of
the god Siva-Nataraja.
$135,000 £60,000

Chinese, Shang/early
Western Zhou dynasty,
bronze pole finial,
15cm. high.
$225,000 £100,000

BRONZE VASES

19th century Japanese bronze vase with Kylin handles, 6½in. high. $45 £20

An Oriental bronze double-handled bottle shaped vase, 9½in. high. $125 £55

A Japanese cloisonne enamel vase in the form of two fish, 14in. high. $180 £80

One of a pair of Japanese bronze bottle shaped vases, 37cm. high. $350 £155

Japanese bronze circular jar and cover. $360 £160

One of a pair of late 19th century bronze vases, 9½in. high. $475 £210

Large late 19th century Komin bronze vase, 19¼in. high. $790 £350

Japanese bronze vase of waisted square shape. $945 £420

Bronze vase and cover, circa 1900, 15½in. high. $1,000 £455

Splashed gilt bronze vase, Chinese, 18th century, 29.5cm. high. $1,195 £530

Late 19th century bronze vase, 17¼in. high. $1,195 £530

5th-3rd century B.C. bronze zhi, 5¾in. high. $1,350 £600

Late 19th century bronze vase, 20¾in. high. $1,530 £680

One of a pair of late 19th century bronze vases, 24¼in. high. $1,855 £825

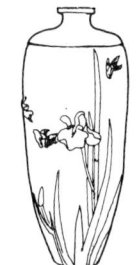

Japanese bronze vase, signed by Dai Nihon Kyoto ju Bunryu. $3,040 £1,350

Gilt splashed bronze vase with trumpet neck, Chinese, 18th century. $3,825 £1,700

One of a pair of Kintani inlaid bronze vases and stands, 116.2cm. high. $10,690 £4,750

One of a pair of Komai style bronze vases, 17½in. high. $11,250 £5,000

A Japanese lacquered miniature cabinet, with three drawers, cupboard and lidded compartments, 15in. high, 11½in. wide. $70 £30

A Persian chest shaped box with lion's paw feet, inlaid with ivory over a tortoiseshell ground, circa 1900. $145 £65

Japanese black lacquered octagonal work box with hinged cover, 15½in. wide. $170 £75

19th century Oriental carved wood games box. $170 £75

A 19th century Chinese yellow lacquer miniature cabinet, enclosed by two doors, on stand. $170 £75

A Kashmir lacquered box. $180 £80

Miniature Japanese cabinet in lacquer, with bird designs. $190 £85

Early 19th century lacquer games box with six lidded boxes and nine trays. $225 £100

A late 19th century Indian ivory inlaid dressing box, the rim crossbanded in ivory and ebony, 17in. wide. $260 £115

Small square Oriental box in the Komai style, late 19th century. $305 £135

19th century Japanese lacquer box. $340 £150

19th century Indonesian casket inlaid with bone, 20in. long. $405 £180

Two-tiered Japanese lacquer picnic box, 25in. wide. $450 £200

Lacquered work box with lift-up lid and four drawers. $565 £250

Large 19th century Chinese carved red lacquer box and cover, 15in. diam. $485 £220

19th century lacquer Suzuribako, 9¼in. wide. $565 £250

Persian lacquered pen box. $925 £420

19th century Japanese Suzuribako with fitted tray. $1,040 £460

BOXES

A Komai type casket from the early 20th century.
$1,530 £680

Late 18th century octagonal lacquer Kojubako, signed Zohiko.
$1,690 £750

Japanese, 19th century lacquered wood box and cover inscribed Shiomi Masanari, 17.3cm. long.
$1,945 £900

Inside lid of a Suzuribako (writing box) lacquered in gold.
$5,290 £2,350

Mid 19th century Persian pen box decorated with seven large panels of figure subjects.
$6,750 £3,000

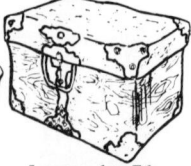

Japanese, late Edo period robe chest (hasami-bako) lacquer with metal mounts, 58.5cm. wide. $7650 £3,400

19th century Japanese rectangular lacquer cabinet, 4in. high.
$8,440 £3,750

Fine Japanese lacquer work box and tray.
$11,250 £5,000

Lacquer pen case in the style of Ali Quli Jabbadar.
$22,500 £10,000

19th century Chinese root carving of an old man. $130 £60

19th century Balinese mask of wood with baked on colours.
$130 £60

A Singalese painted wood panel, 87cm. high. $130 £60

Japanese carved wood figure of a man holding a shoe, 53cm. high.
$155 £70

An Indian carved teak panel with a figure of an elephant in high relief, 69 x 52cm.
$185 £85

A Malayan carved wood kris stand, 18in. high.
$200 £90

Oriental carved double gourd and cover, 16in. high.
$220 £100

Japanese carved wood and black lacquer portable shrine, 5in. high.
$255 £115

An Oriental carved teak jardiniere with flowers, 16in. diam. by 11in. high.
$265 £120

23

CARVED WOOD

Inlaid hardwood panel, circa 1900, 29¾in. long. $240 £110

Late 19th century bronze bell on hardwood stand, 38in. high. $295 £135

A large painted, carved wood kris stand in the form of a grotesque human figure in dancing costume, 22½in. high. $330 £150

A Chinese carved giltwood figure of a Kylon, on a carved gilt and red lacquer stand, 22in. high. $350 £160

Mid 19th century giltwood door frame, 64in. wide. $550 £250

One of a pair of 19th century carved wood temple guardians, 27in. high. $660 £300

Rare Namban figure of a bishop carrying a crozier and rosary, 12in. tall. $900 £400

Persian wood begging bowl. $705 £320

Oriental figure of a Geisha girl with dog. $900 £410

CARVED WOOD

19th century Buddha decorated with gold lacquer, paste and mirror glass.
$925 £420

Late 18th century wood Kyogen mask of Yuzen, 7½in. high.
$1,050 £480

19th century gilt wood figure of Buddha, 20½in. high $1,200 £540

A carved and lacquered figure of a dignitary.
$1,430 £650

Late 19th century gesso and carved wood group, 21in. high.
$1,430 £650

Figure of Amida from the Edo period, in gilt wood, 28¼in. high. $1,760 £800

Late 17th century figure of Budai, in lacquered wood, 22in. high.
$1,925 £875

A Chinese lacquer figure of Wen Chang, the God of Literature, probably of the Sung dynasty, 3ft. high.
$3,520 £1,600

Indian carved and painted wooden elephant.
$5,060 £2,300

25

Porcelain body
Canton decorated
teapot or water
pot. $90 £40

Cantonese polychrome vase
with ovoid body, 18in. high.
$160 £75

19th century Can-
ton enamel mug.
$$200 £90

Small Cantonese
vase. $720 £320

Canton porcelain bowl,
late 19th century,
18¾in. diameter.
$945 £420

A large Cantonese
jardiniere.
$970 £430

One of a pair of late
19th century Canton
altar candlesticks,
7½in. high.
$1,935 £860

One of a pair of yellow
ground Canton porcelain
moonflasks, 47cm. high,
mid 19th century.
$2,025 £900

Louis XV ormolu
mounted Canton ena-
mel bowl decorated
in gilt, 6in. high.
$3,040 £1,350

CANTON

CHINA

One of a pair of late
19th century Canton
porcelain vases in
famille rose enamels,
22¼in. high.
$3,375 £1,500

One of a pair of late
19th century Canton
porcelain garden
seats, 18½in. high.
$5,625 £2,500

One of a pair of
Cantonese vases,
34½in. high.
$7,875 £3,500

CHENGHUA

Chenghua period
(1465-87) porce-
lain vase decorated
in underglaze blue,
8.6cm.
$36,000 £16,000

Chenghua period
porcelain bowl
decorated in under-
glaze blue, 5.6cm.
diameter.
$56,250 £25,000

Doucai wine cup
decorated in blue,
red, yellow and
pale green, with six
character marks of
Chenghua.
$135,000 £60,000

Chenghua stem
cup decorated in
iron red and under-
glaze blue, 4in.
high.
$157,500 £70,000

Chinese porcelain
jar of the Cheng-
hua period, deco-
rated in under-
glaze blue, 10.3cm.
$225,000 £100,000

Blue and white por-
celain saucer dish
from the reign of
Chenghua, 8in.
diameter.
$506,250 £225,000

One of ten wine
cups in Chinese
taste, 2½in. diam.
$170 £75

Guanyao compressed
jar, 4¼in. high.
$225 £100

Zhou dynasty cloth
molded bowl, 3½in.
diam. $900 £400

Fine Wucai baluster
vase and cover, circa
1650-70, 14in. high.
$1,405 £625

18th century blanc-
de-chine figure of
Guanyin, 14in.
high. $1,485 £660

One of a pair of
apple-green Chin-
ese porcelain
vases, 13¾in. high.
$1,630 £725

16th/17th century Yi
dynasty Korean non-
agonal pear shaped
bottle, 11in. high.
$2,100 £935

Sui dynasty straw
glazed equestrian
tomb figure, 13in.
high.$2,250 £1,000

Rare Longquan
fluted baluster jar
and cover, 10¼in.
high. $3,600 £1,600

A rare Chinese Ding-yao bottle from the 11th century A.D., 11¾in. high.
$22,500 £10,000

Rare 14th century Yuan dynasty stem cup stand, 7½in. diam.
$30,000 £14,000

Sung dynasty jar decorated with three stylised leaf sprays, 5¼in.
$37,125 £16,500

15th century Chinese dish in blue and white porcelain, 17in. diam.
$45,000 £20,000

15th century Chinese bowl in blue and white porcelain, 10¾in. diam.
$75,375 £33,500

A Chinese biscuit crouching leopard, almost 21in. high.
$112,500 £50,000

Chinese wine ewer, 14th century, painted in copper red, 12¾in.
$506,250 £225,000

A fine Chinese porcelain moon flask.
$540,000 £240,000

Mid 14th century Chinese wine jar.
$675,000 £300,000

Baluster shaped
porcelain vase,
Daoguang
period, 7¼in.
$80 £35

A Daoguang hexagonal
tureen and cover painted
in underglaze blue, 21cm.
wide. $225 £100

One of a pair of famille rose
vases, possibly Daoguang
reign, 21.8cm. high.
$345 £160

One of a pair of ruby ground
vases and covers of the Daoguang period. $620 £275

Small famille rose
ruby ground bowl,
Daoguang mark.
$730 £325

Chinese porcelain
orchid vase of
the Daoguang
period.
$790 £350

Daoguang blue and
white circular sweet-
meat dish and cover,
13½in. diameter.
$1,530 £680

Late Daoguang fam-
ille rose oviform vase,
12in. high. $1,195 £530

Figure of a recumbent
water buffalo, Jiajing/Dao-
guang, 23cm. long.
$3,600 £1,600

Famille rose plate,
18th century, 9in.
diam. $115 £50

Mid 19th century
famille rose ovi-
form vase, 17in.
high. $315 £140

Famille rose porce-
lain plate, 8¾in.
diameter, late 18th
century.$675 £300

One of a pair of
late famille rose
ormolu mounted
wall vases, 6¼in.
high. $720 £320

Two late 19th century
famille rose figures,
23¾in. high. $1,240 £550

Late 19th century
famille rose vase,
one of a pair, 22in.
high.$1,600 £715

One of a pair of mas-
sive famille rose vases,
36in. high.
           $7,875 £3,500

18th century famille
rose fish tank, 23in.
diam. $9,000 £4,000

A fine famille rose
stylised elephant.
$41,625 £18,500

31

CHINA
FAMILLE VERTE

A Kangxi baluster
vase, decorated in
the famille verte style,
11½in. $340 £150

Late 19th century
famille verte dish,
16in. high.
$500 £230

A famille verte
tea caddy.
$675 £300

Large famille verte
teapot and cover,
10½in. high.
$900 £400

Transitional famille
verte oviform jar,
circa 1660, 24in.
high $1,270 £565

One of a pair of late
17th century famille
verte porcelain fig-
ures. $1,350 £600

Famille verte cylindrical
jardiniere, 24in. diam.
$1,400 £625

One of a pair of
famille verte brush-
washers and water
droppers.
$1,800 £800

Massive famille verte
baluster vase, 33in.
high. $3,825 £1,700

Han dynasty green
glazed pear shaped
vase, 16in. high.
$1,800 £800

Rare green glazed
model of a stove
of the Han dynasty.
$2,250 £1,000

A rare Han dynasty
green glazed well
bucket, 9½in.
$2,600 £1,200

Han dynasty un-
glazed vase, 15½in.
high. $2,700 £1,250

Han dynasty un-
glazed pottery
triceratops, 10½in.
long. $3,600 £1,600

Chinese green glazed
pottery dog of the
Han dynasty, 13½in.
long. $7,875 £3,500

Chinese Han dynasty figure
of a court attendant with
detachable head, 68.6cm.
high. (206BC - AD220)
$34,000 £15,500

Chinese Han dynasty
figure of a lady,
58.5cm. high.
$54,000 £24,000

Grey pottery
ram's head of
the Han dynasty.
$168,750 £75,000

A 19th century
Imari china bowl,
9in. diam. $65 £30

An Imari fluted
baluster vase
decorated with
flowers, 30.5cm.
high. $130 £60

One of a set of
seven 19th cen-
tury Imari shell
dishes.$180 £80

Late 17th century
Imari beaker vase,
15in. high.
        $675 £300

Japanese Imari barber's
bowl, 11in. diameter.
        $1,400 £625

Imari porcelain
goldfish bowl,
20in. diameter.
$2,025 £900

One of a set of
three Imari vases
and covers.
    $2,085 £925

Late 18th century
Imari shallow bowl,
21½in. diameter.
    $6,190 £2,750

Japanese, 17th cen-
tury vase in Arita
porcelain, enamelled
in the Kakiemon
style, 21.5cm.
$28,125 £12,500

Jiajing famille rose bowl enamelled with the 'Immortals from the Isles of the Blest', 56cm. diam.
$3,375 £1,500

A superb Jiajing fish bowl with dragon design, 15½in. high. $6,750 £3,000

A Jiajing vase decorated with yellow dragons on a coral background, 12¼in.
$275,000 £125,000

KAKIEMON

Late 17th century Kakiemon wine pot and cover of ovoid form. $505 £225

A fine teabowl and saucer painted in the Kakiemon palette, circa 1770.
$565 £250

Pair of enamelled Kakiemon tigers seated on rock work, 25cm. high, late 17th century.
$28,125 £12,500

Late 17th century Kakiemon ewer painted in red, blue and green enamels. $39,375 £17,500

Fine early Kakiemon bottle decorated in green and blue enamel, late 17th century, 28.6cm. high.
$58,500 £26,000

Late 17th century Japanese porcelain bowl, Kakiemon, 24.3cm. diameter.
$123,750 £55,000

Small Kangxi tea-
bowl with floral
decoration.
$125 £55

Kangxi blue and white
saucer dish, 14in. diam.
$450 £200

Baluster form porce-
lain vase of powder
blue ground, Kangxi
period, 14¼in. high.
high. $845 £375

Blue and white por-
celain vase of the
Kangxi period,
18¼in. high.
$1,295 £575

Kangxi purple glazed
night light, 8in. high.
$1,350 £600

Kangxi period
group of two
boys, enamelled
in colours, 27.5cm.
high. $7,315 £3,250

One of a pair of
Kangxi pear shaped
bottle vases.
$8,550 £3,800

Kangxi period porce-
lain Monteith vase,
28cm. wide.
$10,125 £4,500

One of a pair of game-
cocks in Chinese porce-
lain, Kangxi period,
10½in. high.
$146,250 £65,000

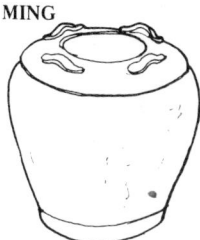

Provincial Ming
stoneware pot
with four lugs,
10in. high.
$265 £120

Late Ming dynasty blue and
white Swatow dish, 41.9cm.
diam. $570 £250

Green glazed pottery ridge-
tile, 11in. high, Ming
dynasty. $620 £275

One of a pair of Ming
pottery joss-stick bur-
ners, 7in. high.
$900 £400

Jiajing Ming blue
and white double
gourd vase, 11in.
high.
$2,250 £1,000

Ming dynasty figure of
Guandi, God of War.
$15,750 £7,000

16th century Ming
jar in blue and white
porcelain, 15in.
diameter.
$29,250 £13,000

Early Ming blue and
white Meiping with
cover, 10¾in. high.
$270,000 £120,000

Early Ming blue and
white porcelain flask,
10in. high.
$303,750 £135,000

37

CHINA
NANKIN

Blue and white
Nankin tankard,
circa 1790, 4½in.
high. $160 £70

A large Nankin serv-
ing dish and cover
in blue and white
porcelain.
$340 £150

A late 18th cen-
tury Nankin por-
celain supper set,
in blue and white,
circa 1780.
$400 £180

Nankin tureen
and cover, circa
1900.
$750 £340

One of a pair of
round blue and
white Nankin
vases, 24in. high.
$1,125 £500

Nankin tureen, deco-
rated in polychrome
and with a domed
cover.
$1,520 £675

ORIENTAL

19th century Orien-
tal teapot decorated
with landscapes in
rust, blue and gilt,
15.5cm. wide.
$135 £60

Two 19th century Orien-
tal baskets. $285 £130

Oriental pottery
jar, 11in. high.
$1,800 £815

A Qianlong figure of a crouching Buddhistic lion, 11¾in. high. $170 £75

Qianlong porcelain rose bowl, 15½in. diam., on hardwood stand. $450 £200

A good Qianlong period 'Tobacco Leaf' teapot. $1,400 £625

Qianlong famille rose octagonal plate, 8½in. wide. $1,350 £600

Qianlong famille rose figure of a court lady, 41cm. high. $2,900 £1,350

One of a pair of Qianlong Compagnie-des-Indes water buffalo tureens and covers. $11,250 £5,000

Chinese porcelain vase of the Qianlong period, decorated with coloured enamels, 16cm. high. $54,000 £24,000

Export tureen modelled as a seated goose, Qianlong, 15¾ x 12¾in. wide. $67,500 £30,000*

One of a pair of Chinese porcelain pheasants, of the Qianlong period, 33cm. $191,250 £85,000

Late 19th century Satsuma pottery vase decorated with figures, 8½in. high.
$35 £15

19th century Satsuma jardiniere decorated with figure scenes, 26cm. diam.
$115 £50

One of a pair of Satsuma baluster vases decorated with heads, 24cm. high. $225 £100

One of a pair of Satsuma vases, 19th century, 7½in. high.
$675 £300

Satsuma jardiniere and stand, 3ft. tall.
$1,125 £500

Satsuma vase, 10in. high, in short necked baluster shape.
$1,270 £565

19th century Satsuma figure of a schoolgirl, 72.5cm. high.
$3,600 £1,600

Fine pair of Satsuma vases, 28in. high.
$4,165 £1,850

One of a pair of large late 19th century Satsuma vases, 68in. high.
$9,450 £4,200

Tang dynasty buff
pottery recumbent
ram, 6¼in. long.
    $1,540 £685

Tang dynasty glazed
pottery amphora,
11in. high.
    $1,970 £875

Tang dynasty brown
glazed figure of a
dog, 6in. high.
    $3,930 £1,745

Tang dynasty rare un-
glazed figure of a camel
groom, 16in. high.
    $6,750 £3,000

A Tang amber glazed
pottery figure of a
Bactrian camel, 16½in.
high. $8,440 £3,750

Tang dynasty dark
green globular stor-
age jar, 7¼in. high.
    $11,250 £5,000

Chinese Tang dynasty
pottery horse with
dwarf riding.
    $12,940 £5,750

Pottery tomb figure
of the Tang dynasty,
13¼in. high.
    $42,000 £19,000

Tang terracotta
horse with high
quality glaze, 72cm.
high. $180,000 £80,000

CHINA
WANLI

A 19th century copy of a Wanli baluster vase decorated in underglaze blue. $65 £30

Wanli blue and white saucer dish, 15in. diam.
$2,590 £1,150

Chinese porcelain bowl, Wanli period, in a European silver gilt mount of about 1600, 14¾in. high.
$45,000 £20,000

WEI

Wei dynasty unglazed pottery hound, 6½in. wide.$1,295 £575

One of two early Wei dynasty pottery tomb attendants.
$1,465 £650

Early Wei dynasty pottery figures of four tomb attendants, 8in. high.
$3,150 £1,400

YIXING

Early 19th century Yixing teapot and cover.
$190 £85

18th century Yixing teapot and cover.
$200 £90

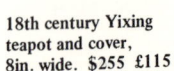

18th century Yixing teapot and cover, 8in. wide. $255 £115

Yongzheng famille rose porcelain plate decorated with blossom, fish, and flowers, 8¾in. diameter.
$675 £300

Yongzheng monochrome brush pot, 4in. high.
$510 £225

Rear view of Chinese Yongzheng period saucer dish, one of a pair, circa 1723-36.
$1,690 £750

Famille rose saucer dish decorated with equestrian warriors from the Yongzheng period. $1,600 £715

One of a pair of Yongzheng famille rose dishes, 12½in. diam.
$4,275 £1,900

One of a pair of Yongzheng famille rose fish bowls.
$8,100 £3,600

One of a pair of jars and covers of the Yongzheng period, 63.5cm. high.
$18,000 £8,000

One of a pair of Yongzheng period bowls painted in the Guyuexuan style, 12.2cm. diam. $40,500 £18,000

Chinese Yongzheng period saucer dish, 51cm. diameter.
$40,500 £18,000

19th century Chinese fire clock, 6.25cm. long. $1,100 £500

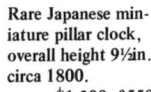

Rare Japanese miniature pillar clock, overall height 9½in., circa 1800. $1,200 £550

Japanese wall clock in ebonised case, 20in. high. $1,700 £780

Japanese brass clock contained in a hardwood cabinet with glazed panels, 12.5cm. high. $2,000 £925

Japanese weight driven wall timepiece, 16in. high. $2,250 £1,000

Porcelain mounted carriage clock, 6½in. high. $3,375 £1,500

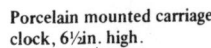

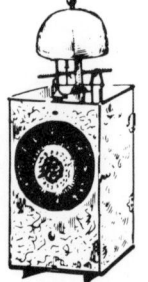

19th century Japanese brass striking bracket clock, 165mm. high. $3,940 £1,750

18th century Japanese lantern clock, 280mm. high. $4,275 £1,900

A Japanese striking bracket clock, 170mm. high. $6,750 £3,000

Late 19th century
small cloisonne
teapot.
$130 £60

19th century Japanese
cloisonne dish, 14in.
diam. $170 £75

20th century clois-
onne enamel box,
5in. wide.
$225 £100

Kin Luong clois-
onne enamel
circular deep
dish, 17¾in. diam.
$280 £125

One of a pair of
cloisonne enamel
shallow bowls,
6in. diam.
$280 £125

A large lidded clois-
onne bowl of cir-
cular shape, banded
with cloud collars,
13½in. diameter.
$280 £125

Japanese cloisonne
enamel jardiniere,
32cm. diameter.
$430 £190

Ovoid cloisonne jar
and cover, circa
1900, one of a pair,
8½in. high.
$550 £250

19th century clois-
onne Koro and
cover, 11½in. high.
$550 £250

CLOISONNE

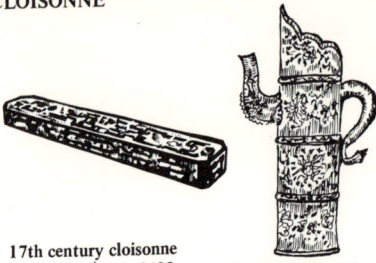

17th century cloisonne
pen rest. $900 £400

Unusual early 19th cen-
tury ewer and cover in
cloisonne, 18½in. high.
$1,350 £625

18th century bronze
and Chinese enamel
figure of Guanyin,
56cm. $1,900 £845

Large 19th century
Japanese cloisonne
enamel dish, 36in.
diam. $2,250 £1,000

A good late 18th
century cloisonne
enamel teapot.
$2,250 £1,000

One of a pair of
Qianlong cloisonne
enamel boxes and
covers, 7in. wide.
$2,250 £1,000

One of a pair of clois-
onne enamel pricket
candlesticks, 19in.
high. $2,250 £1,000

A pair of fine cloisonne
enamel circular trays of
the Qianlong period.
$2,700 £1,200

One of a pair of
Chinese cloisonne
enamel three-branch
candelabra, 42cm.
high. $3,600 £1,600

One of a pair of
Chinese cloisonne
enamel quail.
$565 £250

One of a pair of
late 19th century
Chinese cloisonne
bears. $695 £310

One of a pair of clois-
onne Buddhist lions,
8in. high. $1,100 £500

Cloisonne enamel
quail, 5in. high,
Qianlong period.
$1,150 £525

Pair of Japanese metal-
ware quails in copper,
Shakudo and gilt,
12cm. high.
$1,250 £575

A pair of Chinese
cloisonne enamel
cranes.
$1,465 £650

One of a pair of
cloisonne enamel
seated bulls, 9in.
wide.
$2,815 £1,250

One of a pair of clois-
onne enamel figures
of cocks, 6¾in. high.
$2,900 £1,300

One of a pair of clois-
onne enamel vases,
11in. high, Qianlong
period.
$10,000 £4,500

CLOISONNE VASES

Late 19th century enamel vase of yellow ground, 10in. high. $150 £65

19th century Japanese cloisonne enamel vase, 7in. high. $185 £85

One of a pair of Chinese 12in. cloisonne enamel covered vases. $550 £245

One of a pair of 19th century ormolu mounted cloisonne enamel vases. $755 £335

One of a pair of late 19th century Gu cloisonne vases, 8¾in. high. $760 £340

One of a pair of cloisonne enamel vases, 7½in. high. $945 £430

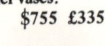

An 18th century Chinese cloisonne vase, 11½in. tall. $1,150 £510

One of a pair of large 19th century vases, 24in. high. $1,710 £760

One of a pair of cloisonne vases, royal blue on powder blue, circa 1860. $2,250 £1,000

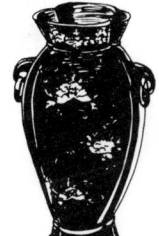

One of a pair of iron-
bodied cloisonne ena-
mel and gilded metal
vases, 22cm. high.
$2,250 £1,000

Cloisonne enamel
vase, 14½in. high,
Wanli period.
$2,250 £1,000

Qianlong cloisonne
enamel flower vase,
12½in. high.
$2,500 £1,100

One of a pair of Japan-
ese cloisonne enamel
vases, 36in. high, circa
1900. $2,600 £1,150

Fine 19th century clois-
onne two-handled vase,
22in. high. $2,650 £1,200

One of a pair of
Chinese cloisonne
vases, 31in. high.
$3,000 £1,400

Kangxi cloisonne
enamel Gu, 13in.
high. $3,300 £1,500

One of a pair of
gold and Shibayama
triform vases, 9in.
high. $4,250 £2,000

Large Japanese
cloisonne enamel
vase, 50in. high.
$6,300 £2,800

COPPER AND BRASS

Eastern brass
bell and brass
wall bracket.
$35 £15

Victorian Benares
ware brass jardiniere.
$45 £20

Two Eastern brass
circlets. $55 £25

Oriental copper
circular tray with
wavy border.
$55 £25

An Indian brass oblong
double-handled tray,
19in. wide. $65 £30

An Oriental cop-
per teapot.
$65 £30

An Indian brass
lidded jug.
$65 £30

A 19th century Orien-
tal brass vase, engraved
with dragons, 12in.
high. $75 £35

Oriental copper
and brass jug.
$75 £35

A Chinese brass
baluster shaped
vase and cover,
11½in. high.
$75 £35

Oriental copper and
silverised jug with
dragon's head handle,
13in. high. $110 £50

Heavy 19th century
Oriental brass spirit
kettle supported by
two monkeys, on a
stand complete with
burner. $110 £50

One of a pair of
Oriental copper
and brass vases.
$145 £65

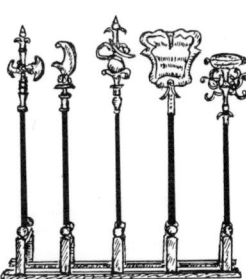

Set of five Chinese ceremonial
maces, 65½in. wide.
$825 £375

Early Qianlong gilt
copper wine ewer,
one of a pair, 12¾in.
high. $1,500 £700

18th century Nepalese
copper and silver figure
of Vajravarahi, 6¼in.
high. $2,150 £950

Persian rose water set, circa 1880,
made in enamelled copper.
$100,000 £45,000

CORAL

Carved coral figure of a lady, 7½in. high, on wood stand.
$650 £300

Coral maiden immortal, 4½in. high, on wood stand.
$875 £400

Carved coral group, 6½in. high, on wood stand.
$925 £420

Coral figure of a goddess, 6¼in. high, on wood stand. $925 £420

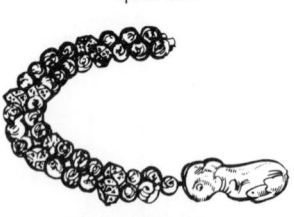
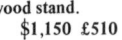

Chinese necklace of finely pierced hollow coral prayer beads, interspersed with silver gilt beads.
$1,000 £450

Coral Guanyin, 8in. high, on wood stand.
$1,150 £510

COSTUME

A mandarin robe of terracotta silk.
$320 £145

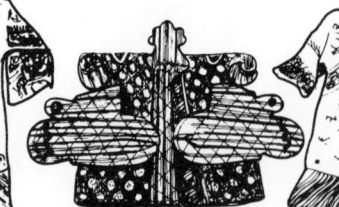
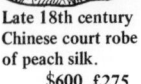

A scarce Indian fabric Cuirass, with two arm pieces, the quilted jacket border with mauve velvet. $330 £150

Late 18th century Chinese court robe of peach silk.
$600 £275

52

A Burmese carved
teak circular jar-
diniere stand, the
pedestal with carved
figure of a bird, 2ft.
9in. high. $200 £90

19th century black
lacquer and gilt
jardiniere.
$460 £210

A Burmese carved
teak davenport with
panel back, on bird
and animal supports.
$660 £330

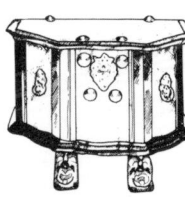

Early 18th century
Sinhalese hardwood
and ebony wine
cooler, 2ft.7in. wide.
$1,090 £485

Fine 19th century
japanned pedestal
desk, 3ft.10in. wide.
$1,150 £500

Late 19th century
bed with cupboards
in frieze, 90in. wide.
$1,900 £865

Late 18th century
lacquer chest, 26in.
wide.$3,900 £1,750

An inlaid Goanese
padouk wood chest
on stand, the legs
formed of skirted
figures. $5,300 £2,400

Late Edo period
Japanese Hasami-
bako, 64.5cm. wide.
$7,900 £3,600

53

FURNITURE
CABINETS

Table cabinet in black, gilt and red lacquer, circa 1880, 26½in. high. $340 £155

Small 19th century Japanese lacquered cabinet of five drawers, 30cm. wide. $340 £155

Modern rosewood side cabinet, 73in. high. $475 £215

Early 20th century rosewood table shrine, 33in. high. $1,065 £485

Black japanned cabinet on stand with cabriole legs, 63in. high. $1,600 £740

Mid 19th century black lacquer shrine, 2ft.11in. x 2ft.8in. $1,850 £850

Early 19th century Chinese carved hardwood altar piece, 46½in. wide. $1,850 £850

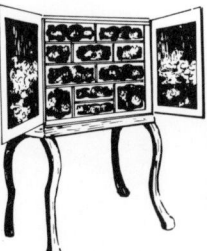

Japanese black lacquer and gilt cabinet, 39in. wide. $2,000 £900

Early 19th century Chinese red lacquer cupboard, 3ft.1½in. wide. $2,000 £900

One of a pair of
Chinese cabinets
with '100 boys'
motif. $2,400 £1,100

An Oriental lacquered
and decorated cabinet,
enclosed by two panel
doors on 37in. stand.
$2,600 £1,200

Early 19th century
Chinese export lac-
quer work cabinet
on paw feet.
$2,900 £1,350

Early 19th century
Chinese export lac-
quer bureau cabinet,
33in. wide.
$3,200 £1,450

Chinese cabinet
with finely figured
burr veneers.
$3,300 £1,500

One of a pair of Chin-
ese 'Bridal' cabinets.
$3,500 £1,600

Early 18th century
Japanese lacquer
cabinet on stand,
40¾in. wide.
$10,000 £4,500

19th century Japanese
black lacquered cabi-
net on stand, 36in.
wide. $15,000 £7,250

Late George III maho-
gany cabinet inset with
18th century Chinese
mirror paintings.
$15,000 £7,250

Child's Chinese
bamboo chair,
circa 1880.
$135 £60

Edwardian corner
chair decorated in
the Chinese style.
$145 £65

19th century Orien-
tal hardwood chair
inlaid with bone and
ivory. $220 £100

An Oriental carved
and pierced circle
back easy chair on
scroll legs. $265 £120

A 19th century Chinese
dragon carved rocking
chair. $395 £175

Rosewood and mother-
of-pearl inlaid arm chair,
circa 1880. $475 £215

One of a pair of
Chinese padouk
wood elbow chairs.
$675 £300

19th century Chinese
teak wood conserva-
tory stool, 21in. high.
$675 £300

One of a set of four 20th century Carine parquetry armchairs. $1,010 £450

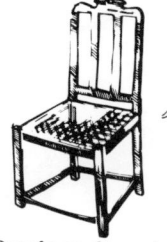

One of a set of ten maho-
gany dining chairs, 18th/
19th century, possibly
Anglo-Chinese.
$1,125 £500

Unusual Indian teak
piano stool, circa
1900. $1,180 £525

19th century Korean
cinnabar lacquer and
gilded open armchair
with leather seat.
$1,350 £600

One of two carved
and ebonised Orien-
tal chairs.
$1,430 £650

A late 18th century
Indo-Portugese
padouk wood bur-
gomaster chair.
$1,400 £650

One of a set of four Chinese
mother-of-pearl inlaid rosewood open armchairs.
$2,025 £900

One of a pair of 17th
century Chinese hard-
wood hoop backed
chairs. $3,935 £1,750

One of ten late 19th century
Chinese chairs in marble and
rosewood. $4,610 £2,050.

One of three silver moun-
ted arm chairs, part of a
set of Indian late 19th
century furniture, inclu-
ding a settee and stool.
$33,750 £15,000

FURNITURE
DISPLAY CABINETS

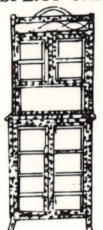

Unusual Oriental bamboo china cabinet, circa 1900.
$400 £180

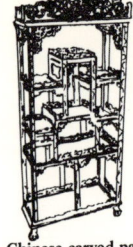

Chinese carved padouk wood etagere, 2ft.6in. wide.
$715 £325

Late 19th century hardwood etagere, 63in. high.
$990 £450

19th century ivory mounted display cabinet, 39in. wide.
$1,000 £450

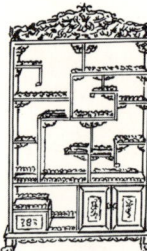

Late 19th century stained rosewood side cabinet, 76in. high. $1,210 £550

Late 19th century walnut and rosewood display cabinet.
$1,400 £625

19th century Japanese black lacquered display cabinet, 37in. wide. $2,250 £1,000

Oriental carved hardwood display cabinet.
$2,640 £1,200

Japanese padouk cabinet.
$2,700 £1,250

19th century Orien-
tal lacquered display
cabinet with ivory
mounts.
$2,600 £1,200

A late 19th century
Japanese padouk wood
porcelain cabinet on
stand, 7ft. high.
$2,600 £1,200

Fine Oriental hard-
wood cabinet, gold
panels with ivory
carvings, 48in. wide.
$3,200 £1,450

Fine Oriental cabi-
net with ivory
panels, 46in. wide.
$3,740 £1,700

Late 19th century
Japanese display
cabinet.
$3,740 £1,700

18th century Chinese
lacquered cabinet,
decorated with dom-
estic scenes.
$5,250 £2,400

Late 19th century
small display cabi-
net, 48in. high.
$6,270 £2,850

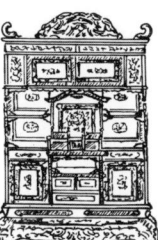

19th century hardwood
and ivory mounted dis-
play cabinet.
$6,820 £3,100

Japanese lacquered
Sho-Dana with sil-
ver mounts.
$11,000 £5,000

FURNITURE SCREENS

Late 19th century Japanese carved two-fold screen, 70in. high. $235 £105

19th century Oriental carved teak three-fold screen. $220 £100

Japanese ivory table screen, 12½in. high. $495 £220

Late 19th century red lacquer two-fold screen, 71¼in. high. $540 £240

Late 19th century Chinese three-fold screen, one of a pair. $675 £300

Japanese carved and ebonised four-leaf draught screen, 6ft. 3in. high. $675 £300

Victorian carved hardwood Chinese screen with floral decoration. $725 £330

Late 19th century hardwood four-fold screen, 73in. high. $875 £400

Japanese ivory table screen, 16½in. high. $1,300 £600

20th century Qianlong six-fold coromandel screen, 72½in. high. $1,750 £800

A late Victorian carved coromandel wood screen with lacquered decoration of birds and foliage. $2,200 £1,000

Two-fold lacquer and ivory screen, circa 1900. $2,250 £1,000

20th century Qianlong six-fold screen, 72½in. high. $2,475 £1,100

An ivory, mother-of-pearl and Shibayama two-fold screen, 64in. high. $2,475 £1,100

18th century Chinese draught screen, 1.88m. high. $6,750 £3,000

Early 19th century Chinese export black and gold lacquer eight-leaf screen. $7,150 £3,250

Part of a large 19th century Chinese eight-leaf screen. $9,250 £4,200

Kengoku grained lacquer two-fold screen, late 19th century. $20,000 £9,000

61

FURNITURE
SETTEES

19th century Oriental hardwood highly carved settee. $565 £260

19th century, highly carved, Burmese teak double ended chaise longue, decorated with animals and scrolls. $675 £310

Highly carved 19th century hardwood settee with intertwined dragon back. $810 £360

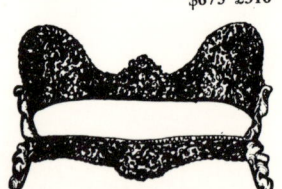

Burmese settee of serpentine shape extensively carved and pierced. $1,015 £450

A Moresque hardwood double seat, with tortoiseshell and mother-of-pearl inlay. $1,070 £475

Late 19th century rosewood and mother-of-pearl inlaid settee. $1,575 £700

Late 19th century mother-of-pearl inlaid hardwood settee, circa 1880, 6ft.7in. long. $1,915 £850

Part of a late 19th century five-piece Burmese hardwood suite, all heavily carved and pierced with dragon designs. $2,000 £900

An Oriental carved
teak, square taper-
ing lamp stand, 4ft.
2in. high. $90 £40

Late 19th century
Oriental hardwood
stand. $120 £55

Chinese carved
padouk wood
jardiniere stand,
2ft. high.$225 £100

Chinese carved hard-
wood square jar-
diniere stand, 18in.
high. $265 £120

A Chinese carved hard-
wood, circular jardin-
iere stand, standing on
square legs, 2ft. high.
            $320 £145

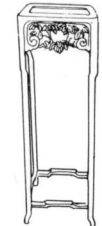

Chinese carved hard-
wood square jardin-
iere stand, 3ft.8in.
high. $330 £150

Round cistern stand
with marble top,
carved legs, frieze
and undershelf.
            $400 £180

Oriental three-tier
hardwood display
stand. $500 £230

One of a pair of
hardwood pedestals,
circa 1900, 51½in.
high. $550 £250

FURNITURE STANDS

A Japanese carved hardwood circular jardiniere stand, 18in. high.
$550 £250

20th century hardwood urn stand, 34in. high.
$585 £265

Late 19th century urn stand in rosewood, 32in. high.
$605 £275

Late 19th century hardwood urn stand, 33½in. high.
$845 £385

One of a pair of Chinese rosewood and mother-of-pearl inlaid urn stands, 41in. high. $945 £430

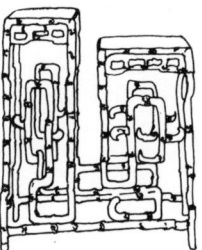

Late 19th century rosewood etagere with two tops.
$1,100 £500

Unusual pagoda, circa 1880, 85½in. high. $1,485 £675

One of a pair of Japanese vase stands, 24in. high.
$6,000 £2,750

Late 17th century Japanese lacquer Sho-Dana.
$14,000 £6,250

Oriental carved black-wood and inlaid circular coffee table on a folding stand, 61cm. diam. $65 £30

A˘Cairo, carved wood, square bedside stand, with hinged top and an undershelf. £75 £35

19th century Bur-mese carved teak wood table with pierced apron, 68cm. diameter.   £135 £60

19th century Indian inlaid games table, 32¼in. wide. $550 £250

19th century hard-wood table inlaid with mother-of-pearl. $650 £300

Burmese padouk wood writing table. $770 £350

19th century Oriental carved teak writing desk.$990 £440

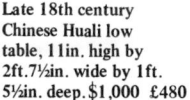

Late 18th century Chinese Huali low table, 11in. high by 2ft.7½in. wide by 1ft. 5½in. deep.$1,000 £480

North African octa-gonal hardwood table, circa 1930. $1,100 £500

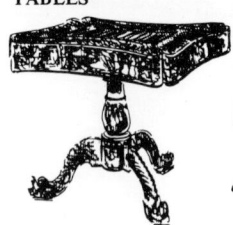

Chinese export black and gilt lacquer games table, circa 1850, 35in. wide.
$1,240 £550

Late 19th century bonheur-du-jour, 48½in. wide.
$1,250 £575

18th century Oriental padouk centre table, 52½ x 23in.
$1,350 £600

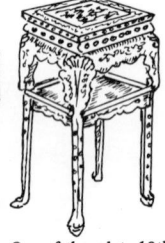

Late 19th century centre table in rosewood, 28½in. high.
$1,350 £600

One of three late 19th century rosewood and mother-of-pearl occasional tables, 31½in. high. $1,800 £800

Chinese padouk wood altar table of the 18th century, 5ft.7in. wide.
$1,915 £850

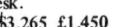

18th century Chinese black lacquer side table.
$2,700 £1,250

Early 20th century Chinese pedestal desk.
$3,265 £1,450

A Chinese padouk wood table profusely inlaid with mother-of-pearl.
$4,500 £2,000

Chinese carved camphorwood chest, 3ft.4in. wide. $185 £85

An Oriental hardwood chest, the top, front and sides carved with extensive landscapes in relief, 4ft. wide. $285 £125

Oriental carved camphorwood chest, 94cm. long. $330 £150

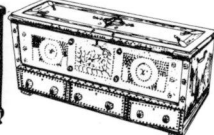

An Oriental elm, iron bound chest, circa 1830. $660 £300

A Celonese brass mounted teak chest, the lid and front applied with pierced and engraved sheet brass and brass studs. $800 £375

A highly carved 19th century camphorwood chest. $825 £375

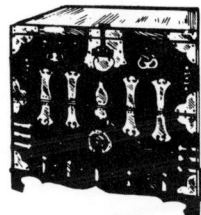

Korean finely engraved brass mounted chest, circa 1870. $945 £430

Korean brass bound elm chest, circa 1870. $1,000 £450

18th century Portugese East Indian chest on stand in padouk wood, 36in. wide. $1,000 £450

GLASS

Qianlong overlay vase.
$790 £360

Qianlong Pekin royal blue glass bottle, 12¼in. high. $1,205 £545

Rare Sidonian bottle, circa 100 A.D.
$1,900 £865

18th century Moghal Indian vessel, the base of a hookah. $2,125 £945

A fine Qianlong red overlay glass vase, 12in. high.
$2,650 £1,200

One of a pair of red overlay glass ginger jars, Qianlong period, 5½in. high.
$3,200 £1,450

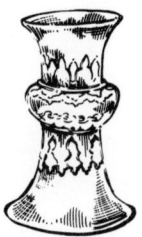

One of a pair of egg yolk yellow Pekin glass beakers, 9½in. high. $10,685 £4,750

14th century two-handled Syrian vase of glass, enamelled in colours, 30.5cm. high. $16,875 £7,500

Mamluk enamelled glass sweetmeat jar and cover.
$36,000 £16,000

68

Rhinoceros horn
libation cup.
$340 £150

Early 18th century
rhinoceros horn
libation cup, 3½in.
high. $675 £300

A fine carved fig-
ure of a rat with
large eyes of
dark horn.
$810 £360

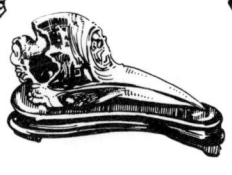

Rhinoceros horn
libation cup.
$1,070 £475

One of a rare pair
of hornbill skulls,
7½in. long.
$1,690 £750

Kangxi rhinoceros
horn libation cup,
4½in. high.
$1,690 £750

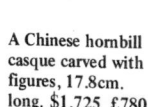

Kangxi rhinoceros
horn libation cup,
4½in. high.
$1,690 £750

A Chinese hornbill
casque carved with
figures, 17.8cm.
long. $1,725 £780

Late 19th century
pair of carved
rhinoceros horns,
25½in. high.
$3,825 £1,700

INROS

Japanese four case inro decorated in red, gold and black lacquer, signed Bunryusai. $270 £120

Late 17th century four case inro, unsigned. $520 £230

Three compartment inro decorated with a pair of silver cranes, signed Koma Kiuhaku. $550 £245

An unsigned 19th century five case inro, decorated in gold hira-maki-e. $570 £260

Three case inro decorated in gold, red, grey and other coloured lacquers, signed Katikawa. $650 £300

19th century gold lacquer four case inro, signed Toyo. $675 £310

19th century three case red lacquer inro. $715 £325

19th century three case red lacquer inro, inlaid with pewter. $750 £340

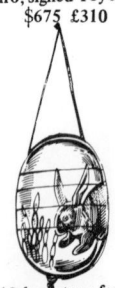

19th century four case inro, inlaid with pewter and aogai. $815 £370

A late Edo period lacquer inro, with sliding panel and three compartments. $925 £420

An inro of the mid Edo period, in the style of Korin, inlaid with mother-of-pearl and oxidised pewter. $945 £430

Fine 19th century Japanes five case gold lacquer inro. $1,000 £450

19th century fine four case lacquer inro, signed Yoy-usai. $1,250 £575

19th century four case lacquer inro. $1,350 £625

An early 19th century five case inro signed Kajikawa. $1,600 £725

A four case inro signed Shokosai, depicting crested and breaking waves. $1,600 £725

19th century five case lacquer inro signed Shohusai Yuho. $1,600 £725

A five case inro signed Kajikawa. $1,745 £775

Black, silver and grey
example of an inro or
multiple belt box.
$1,700 £780

A gold lacquered five
case inro decorated
with metal, pearl
and horn.
$1,750 £800

Late 18th century
five case inro sig-
ned Kajikawa.
$2,000 £900

19th century five
case inro, signed
Kofu. $2,000 £900

Decorated inro or
multiple belt box.
$2,475 £1,100

A six case inro, signed
Koma Kyukaku, with
a netsuke signed Zas-
hin. $2,590 £1,150

A 19th century inro,
signed Jokasi, deco-
rated in gold, black,
red and silver hira-
maki-e. $2,600 £1,150

19th century gold
lacquer inro, sig-
ned Hosensai Sad-
amasa.
$2,600 £1,150

An unsigned four
case inro deco-
rated in gold and
silver tatamaki-e.
$2,700 £1,250

A four case inro, signed Kosai, decorated in gold, red and black lacquer.
$2,925 £1,300

A four case, 19th century inro, signed Kakosai of Shozan.
$3,600 £1,600

A four case Somada style inro decorated with typical Japanese scene.
$4,250 £2,000

A rare three case inro signed Jokasai and Yosei.
$6,030 £2,680

An unusual Japanese inro of triangular shape. $8,440 £3,750

Five case burnished lacquer inro by Kasen.
$9,000 £4,000

Early 19th century Japanese lacquer inro by Shibata Zeshin, 4¾in. long.
$21,375 £9,500

Tachibana Gyokuzan and Suzuki Tokoku inro.
$25,875 £11,500

One of a set of twelve inros showing the Japanese signs of the Zodiac.
$45,000 £20,000

73

INCENSE BURNERS

19th century bronze vase with pierced cover, 6in. $55 £25

A Chinese 19th century bronze incense burner, the domed lid cast and pierced with entwined dragons, 12in. high. $180 £80

18th century Chinese bronze incense burner. $215 £95

Early 19th century Chinese censer with wood and jade lid. $225 £100

19th century Kylin bronze incense burner, 7½in. high. $295 £130

19th century lacquered bronze incense burner. $400 £180

Early 19th century cloisonne enamel incense burner. $755 £355

One of a pair of 19th century Chinese cloisonne, elephant shaped, incense burners, 5½in. high. $1,090 £485

Yuan dynasty celadon incense burner, 3¾in. wide. $1,100 £500

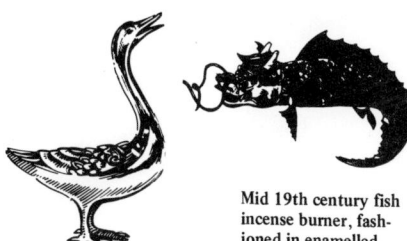

Early 19th century
bronze incense bur-
ner, one of a pair,
10½in. high.
$1,440 £650

Mid 19th century fish
incense burner, fash-
ioned in enamelled
silver with gilt mounts,
20in. wide.
$1,745 £775

Early 18th century
cloisonne enamel
incense burner and
cover, 5¼in. diam.
$1,900 £850

Mottled spinach
jade tripod incense
burner, 7in. wide.
$2,100 £950

Pair of Qianlong
cloisonne incense
burners, each suppor-
ted on gilt bronze
elephant heads, 26in.
high. $2,815 £1,250

Green jade cen-
ser and cover of
the Qianlong
dynasty.
$2,815 £1,250

Pair of Chinese Qian-
long cloisonne enamel
incense burners in the
form of quails, 5¾in.
high. $3,600 £1,600

Early 16th century
Ming cloisonne enamel
incense burner, 11½in.
wide. $4,000 £1,850

19th century chloro-
melanite incense bur-
ner, 8½in. high.
$15,000 £6,750

A 19th century Indo-Persian steel model of a human headed bird, 14¾in. high. $585 £265

Early 20th century inlaid Komei iron dish showing a warrior, 8¾in. diam. $600 £275

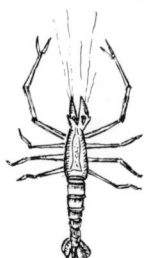

Late 19th century articulated iron crayfish, 9in. long. $715 £325

Unusual 18th or 19th century iron Buddhist travelling shrine. $1,150 £530

Late 19th century inlaid bronze and iron flaming nimbus, 7¼in. high. $1,600 £725

Persian metal figure of a Simurgh, 19th century, 48cm. high. $2,900 £1,350

One of a pair of 19th century Indo-Iranian steel candlesticks with gold inlay, 11¾in. high. $4,500 £2,000

19th century Iranian steel cat with silver and gold harness. $30,000 £13,500

One of a pair of Iranian steel doves, damascened in gold, 9½in. high. $33,750 £15,000

76

Chinese ivory cricket cage containing miniature dominoes, 2½in. high.$34 £15

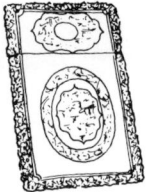

Chinese ivory card case with carved panels. $70 £30

19th century Chinese ivory concentric pierced ball.$110 £50

Chinese ivory figure of a boy with mask, 8cm. high. $115 £50

Chinese ivory figure of a girl holding a fan and a flower, 18.5cm. high. $135 £60

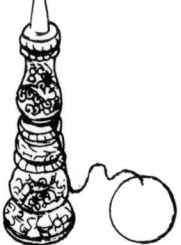

Late 18th century Chinese ivory game of Bilboquet. $146 £65

Oriental ivory head on wooden stand, circa 1900, 5¾in. high. $180 £80

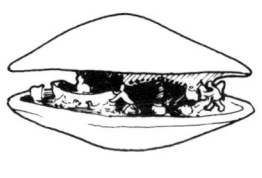

One of a pair of Japanese ivory shells, interiors carved with landscapes. $205 £90

19th century Japanese ivory figure of a sage, 25cm. high. $200 £90

IVORY

Japanese ivory table seal with group of three Kylons. $225 £100

Finely carved and pierced ivory Ryusa netsuke of a Phoenix with kiri leaves and stylised waves.
$225 £100

One of two ivory bottles on wooden stands. $225 £100

Chinese ivory figure of a boy on a see-saw, 17cm. high. $280 £125

19th century carved ivory Okimono.
$305 £135

Late 19th century Okimono style figure of a hunter.
$370 £165

An ivory tusk, carved to show a procession of travellers, 19in.
$405 £180

Chinese ivory figure of a man with musical instruments, 31cm. high. $450 £200

Carved ivory tusk section on a fret stand. $415 £185

Late 19th century
Japanese ivory group,
signed Tomo-Yuki.
$450 £200

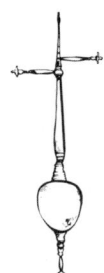

Javanese Pelog Rebab
with head, neck and
tail spike of turned
ivory. $565 £250

Mid 19th century
ivory wrist rest,
Chinese. $565 £250

Marine ivory farmer,
signed Shomei, 11in.
high. $610 £270

19th century ivory Oki-
mono of an umbrella-
maker, signed Soraku.
$610 £270

19th century Japanese
carved ivory figure of
Daruma, signed Haya-
shi, 7¼in. high.
$620 £275

Late 19th century
sectional Japanese
ivory group, 14in.
long. $675 £300

An ivory fowl, 16.5cm.
high. $730 £325

Old man made of
ivory, 12in. high,
on hardwood stand.
$765 £340

A carved ivory fig-
ure of Hotei, Japan-
ese, circa 1900, 5in.
high. $900 £400

One of a pair of Qian-
long ivory fan carvings,
8½in. wide. $900 £400

Japanese tinted
ivory group.
$1,170 £520

Chinese ivory 'Boat
of Happiness'.
$1,240 £550

Tokyo School
ivory carving of
an old man taking
a stroll.
$1,630 £725

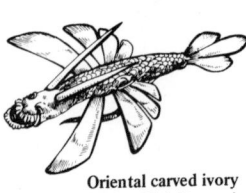

Oriental carved ivory
'Flying Fish Dragon',
15in. long.
$1,630 £725

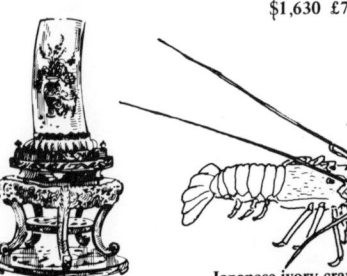

Masayasu Shibayama
ivory tusk vase, circa
1900. $1,630 £725

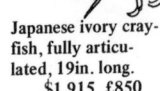

Japanese ivory cray-
fish, fully articu-
lated, 19in. long.
$1,915 £850

Pair of ivory tusks de-
corated with mother-
of-pearl, ivory and
hardstone, on carved
wood stands.
$1,970 £875

17th century Singa-
lese ivory casket,
4in. high.
$2,250 £1,000

19th century Japanese
ivory carving of a travelling salesman carrying
baskets, 10¼in. tall.
$2,475 £1,100

One of a pair of
Japanese carved
ivory tusks.
$2,475 £1,100

Koichi ivory fisher-
man, about 1900,
11¼in. high.
$2,700 £1,200

One of a pair of Chinese
export ivory vases with
silver gilt mounts by J.
Bridge, 1829, 26cm.
high. $3,600 £1,600

Japanese ivory figure of
a girl and a baby, signed
Shugyoku, circa 1900.
$3,600 £1,600

Fine Nobuaki ivory
group, circa 1900,
18.5cm. high.
$3,600 £1,600

Fine ivory carving
of a caparisoned
elephant, 19th cen-
tury.
$4,500 £2,000

Japanese ivory figure
of a mask carver by
Ishikawa Komei,
circa 1900, 9¼in.
high. $7,200 £3,200

JADE

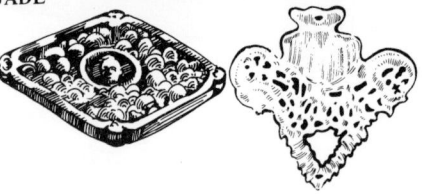

Chinese pale green jade plaque, 2¾in. square. $55 £25

Jade medallion carved and pierced with baskets of flowers and fruit, 2¾in. wide. $120 £55

Small 19th century jade medallion depicting two fish. $130 £60

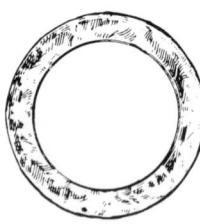

One of a pair of jade circular bangles, 3¼in. diam. $155 £70

A fine Chinese pierced white jade belt clasp with intricately pierced design of a sage seated in a forest. $220 £100

Square mutton fat jade bottle applied with coral. $400 £180

Early 19th century Chinese circular plaque with fine jade figures. $400 £180

Hardstone and jadeite screen on carved hardwood stand, Chinese, circa 1900. $715 £325

Chinese circular jade table screen, 10in. diameter. $900 £400

82

An emerald and white jade pendant, 2½in. high. $2,000 £900

Jade ewer and cover, 7½in. high.
$2,000 £900

A jade axe joined by fibre attachments to a bone handle, 11½in. long. $1,600 £725

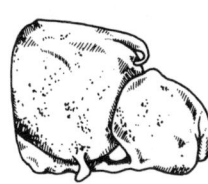

A celadon and rust jade boulder carving, 7¾in. high.
$3,300 £1,500

Translucent jade table screen, 9 x 6¾in.
$6,600 £3,000

18th century jade peach group, 4½in. long. $2,650 £1,200

A Moghul moss green jade stand, 31 x 28cm.
$11,000 £5,000

18th century Chinese jade screen with mutanwood stand.
$22,500 £10,000

Green jade boulder on a gilt metal stand, Kangxi period, 30.5cm. high.
$26,500 £12,000

JADE ANIMALS

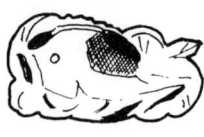

Late 18th century green jade fish, 2¼in. long. $55 £25

Small Chinese jade figure of a monkey. $65 £30

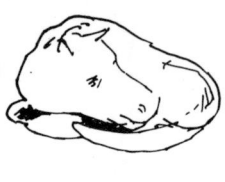

Small mutton fat jade carving of a recumbent horse, Chinese, 2in. wide. $255 £115

18th century carved jade mythical beast, 2in. high. $375 £170

Chinese jade dragon and lizard belt buckle. $850 £400

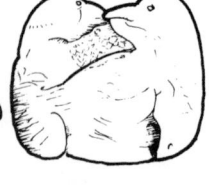

18th century Qing period jade group of two birds, 2½in. wide. $850 £400

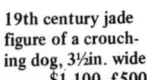

19th century jade figure of a crouching dog, 3½in. wide. $1,100 £500

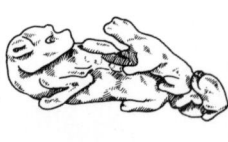

18th century jade Buddhist lion group, 6in. long. $1,350 £600

18th century recumbent chimera in burnt jade. $1,350 £600

84

18th century re-
cumbent chimera
in burnt jade
$1,350 £600

White jade Budd-
hist lion and cub,
3in. long.
$1,450 £650

Ming period jade
figure of a single
horned mythical
beast, 7cm. high.
$1,450 £650

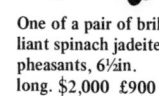

One of a pair of
jadeite parrots,
7in. long.
$1,600 £725

One of a pair of bril-
liant spinach jadeite
pheasants, 6½in.
long. $2,000 £900

A mottled yellow
brown jade chim-
era, 7½in. long.
$2,250 £1,000

A carved jade fab-
ulous animal,
10in. long.
$2,400 £1,100

18th century Chinese
ivory toned jade carv-
ing, veined with a black
design of a carp, 7in.
long. $2,400 £1,100

18th century pale
jade group of a
ram and young,
8cm. long.
$3,750 £1,700

JADE
ANIMALS

18th century jade
figure of a bird
slightly turning its
head, 6½in. long.
$3,700 £1,700

One of a pair of
white jade figures
of a bird with lotus
sprays in its beak,
9in. high.
$3,700 £1,700

18th century jade
carving of a carp
swimming amidst
lotus plants, 9in.
wide.
$3,800 £1,750

Superb jade carv-
ing of mytholo-
gical figures ris-
ing from the sea.
$4,000 £1,800

A flecked pale grey
jade carving of a
recumbent pony,
8½in. long.
$5,250 £2,400

Ming dynasty jade
carving of a pony
and foal, 5¼in.
long.
$17,000 £7,750

A beautiful jade
mottled pony.
$18,500 £8,500

Chinese jade carv-
ing of a twin carp,
made in the reign of
Jiajing, 7½in. long.
$18,500 £8,500

Pale green jade
water buffalo
from the Ming
dynasty, 4½in.
high.
$150,000 £70,000

One of a pair of
Chinese green
jadeite bowls,
5.5cm. diam.
$330 £150

Leys jar in
white jade, 2in.
high.
$900 £400

Pale grey foliate
dish in jade, 7¾in.
diam.
$1,400 £650

Late Qianlong grey-
ish white jade bowl,
5¾in. diam.
$1,650 £750

A white jade pom-
made pot and cover,
2½in. high.
$1,850 £850

One of a pair of
flecked spinach
green jade bowls,
5¾in. wide.
$2,000 £900

Qianlong white pier-
ced jade bowl and
cover, 5in. diam.
$2,400 £1,100

18th century circu-
lar white jade bowl,
5½in. wide.
$2,450 £1,125

Qianlong mottled
white jade Koro and
cover, 6¾in. wide.
$3,500 £1,600

JADE
BOWLS AND DISHES

A pair of Qianlong celadon jade marriage dishes, 5in. diam. $4,000 £1,800

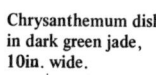

Chrysanthemum dish in dark green jade, 10in. wide.
$5,250 £2,400

Qianlong greyish white jade globular jar and cover.
$5,700 £2,600

Celadon jade Ding, 8¾in. high.
$6,800 £3,100

Large celadon jade bowl, Qianlong, 11½in. wide.
$9,200 £4,200

18th century Chinese bowl of pale celadon jade, 19cm. wide.
$12,000 £5,500

18th century Chinese celadon jade bowl, 23.5cm. wide.
$17,000 £7,800

A fine Qianlong green jade bowl.
$20,000 £9,000

Early 18th century Koro and cover, in pale green jade, 5½in. high.
$30,000 £13,500

Qianlong pale grey
jade brushwasher.
$475 £215

Pale celadon jade
brushwasher,
4¾in. wide.
$1,450 £650

A greyish white
jade brush pot,
5¼in. high.
$2,400 £1,100

Fine quality 18th
century jade brush-
washer.
$2,900 £1,350

Qianlong mottled grey
and russet jade brush-
washer, 6¾in. wide.
$3,150 £1,450

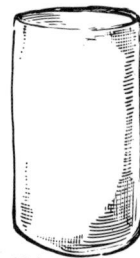

18th century brush
pot in white jade,
3½in. high, sold
with wood stand.
$3,300 £1,500

Qianlong carved and
pierced white jade
brushwasher, 5½in.
wide.
$3,750 £1,700

Chinese brush pot car-
ved with 'The Seven
Sages of the Bamboo
Grove', 1776, in spin-
ach green jade.
$16,000 £7,500

Chinese brush pot
in pale celadon
jade, 14cm. high.
$20,000 £9,000

JADE FIGURES

Chinese jade figure of a man, 2½in. high. $75 £35

Celadon jade figure of a goddess, 9½in. high. $900 £400

Carved jade group of Shoulao, 4½in. high. $1,000 £450

Pale green jade figure of a lady, 12in. high. $1,900 £875

Chinese jade group of two maidens. $2,000 £900

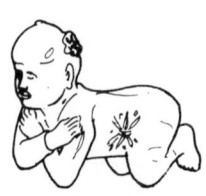

A spinach jade fertility baby pillow, 41 x 48cm. $2,250 £1,000

A Wei dynasty jade carving of Avaldkitesvara. $3,250 £1,500

A pale flecked jade carving of Guanyin standing under a banana tree, 8½in. high. $4,000 £1,800

Large pale celadon jade carving of Guanyin, 14in. high. $4,250 £2,000

Small mutton fat
jade vase and cover,
3½in. high, Chinese.
$220 £100

Pale grey jade hexa-
gonal vase, 4¼in.
high. $540 £245

Unusual jade cov-
ered vase, 5½in.
high. $800 £360

Chinese jade baluster
vase carved with
Phoenix, 7¾in.
high. $1,450 £660

Qianlong celadon jade
Koro and cover, 6½in.
tall. $1,850 £850

Chinese jade vase
in the shape of a
lotus leaf, 5¾in.
high.
    $2,100 £950

Greenish white jade
hanging vase and
cover, 10in. high.
$2,300 £1,050

Qianlong greyish white
double vase and two covers,
6½in. wide. $3,250 £1,500

A greyish celadon
jade archaistic Gu,
8in. high.
$4,000 £1,800

91

A pale grey jade
triple spill vase,
6in. high.
$4,000 £1,800

A pale greyish white
jade archaistic vase,
8in. high.
$4,000 £1,800

18th century pale
celadon jade vase
and cover, 8½in.
high.
$4,600 £2,000

A mottled pale cela-
don jade vase and
cover, 6½in. high.
$5,250 £2,400

One of a pair of early
18th century joss stick
burners, in celadon
jade, 9¾in. high.
$6,750 £3,000

Qianlong fine
white jade vase and
cover, 9½in. high.
$11,000 £5,000

A large spinach green
jade vase and cover,
13½in. high.
$26,000 £12,000

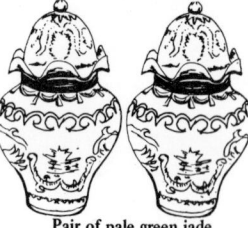

Pair of pale green jade
vases with slight brown
markings, 12in. high.
$26,000 £12,000

A mutton fat jade
vase and cover,
20½in. high.
$40,000 £18,000

Chinese carved figure of a sage, fitted for electric light.
$110 £50

Japanese carved wood hexagonal hanging lantern, 61cm. high.
$110 £50

An Oriental engraved brass oil floor lamp with shade. $225 £100

19th century pottery elephant oil lamp, 24in. high.
$330 £150

One of a pair of lanterns and stands, 17in. high.
$1,800 £800

Qianlong fine white jade vase and cover, 9½in. high.
$2,000 £925

Enamelled mosque lamp decorated in Islamic taste, circa 1870.
$3,000 £1,400

One of a pair of Qianlong ivory lanterns and stands, 15¼in. high.
$3,150 £1,400

A Mamluk enamelled mosque lamp in the name of Sultan Malik Zahir Barkuk, 1382-99.
$25,000 £11,000

MIRRORS

Late 19th century
hardwood and ivory
inlaid mirror.
$550 £250

18th century lacque-
red dressing table
mirror with a fitted
compartment below.
$660 £300

Late 18th century
Indian ivory and
penwork mirror.
$955 £425

Heavily carved early
20th century wall
mirror, 78¾in. high.
$1,250 £550

One of a pair of Chin-
ese Chippendale gilt
wood miniature wall
mirrors. $1,500 £675

19th century Persian mir-
ror with a finely painted
lid signed and dated
1840, 10¼ x 7¼in.
$1,600 £725

Good hardwood
mirror, circa 1880,
70in. high.
$2,400 £1,100

19th century Indian
carved teak mirror.
$3,750 £1,700

A fine Chinese Chip-
pendale wall mirror,
3ft. tall, 2ft.6in. wide.
$8,000 £3,600

Japanese ivory
netsuke of a
man. $100 £45

Carved ivory net-
suke of a stylised
head. $115 £50

Ivory mask
netsuke.
$125 £55

Japanese ivory net-
suke of a gourd
with a horse head.
$135 £60

A carved ivory Ryusa
netsuke with Hotei
seated, two children
and two others on
reverse. $236 £105

Shozan dancer
with open fan,
signed. $250 £110

Ivory netsuke of
Longarms, 3in.
high. $260 £115

18th century ivory
netsuke of a recum-
bent Sennin.
$340 £150

Carved ivory net-
suke of a mouse.
$385 £170

NETSUKE

19th century ivory
netsuke of the three
heroes of Han.
$450 £200

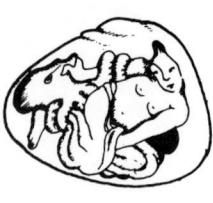

Good carved ivory
Shunga netsuke
signed Vukimasa.
$475 £210

19th century ivory
netsuke of a rat-
catcher, signed
Hansaku.
$475 £210

Ivory netsuke of
the Demon War-
rior on horseback,
1¾in. high.
$505 £225

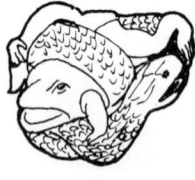

A wooden netsuke of
a toad entwined by
a snake. $530 £240

19th century Japan-
ese carved ivory net-
suke of seven figures
in a boat, signed, 3in.
long. $565 £250

Early 19th cen-
tury ivory net-
suke.
$585 £260

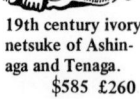

19th century ivory
netsuke of Ashin-
aga and Tenaga.
$585 £260

Unsigned 19th cen-
tury wood netsuke.
$570 £260

Ivory Okimono style netsuke of two Oni, carved with a head of Shoki, signed Gyoku. $620 £275

Carved ivory netsuke of a monkey in a shell. $675 £300

Carved wood netsuke of a monkey with her young, signed Harumi tsu. $730 £325

19th century trick netsuke by Tomomasa. $765 £340

Ivory netsuke of Soki doing battle with four Oni, 2in. high. $810 £360

Ivory netsuke of a mouse in a rope. $945 £420

Netsuke of Tamamo No Mae and the Fox with Nine Tails, 2in. high. $1,070 £475

Standing horse netsuke. $1,070 £475

Netsuke group of a bearded man and an ox, 2in. high. $1,080 £480

Ivory netsuke of
two pups.
$1,125 £500

19th century ivory
netsuke of Ashinaga
and Tenaga by Tom-
oyasu. $1,465 £650

Ivory netsuke of
mushrooms by
Okatomo.
$1,485 £660

Fine ivory netsuke
of a seated dog,
signed Tomotanda.
$1,630 £725

Carved ivory netsuke,
Tomotada School, 2¼in.
long, unsigned Japanese.
$1,575 £700

Ivory netsuke by
Homei.
$1,630 £725

Late 18th century
early 19th century
netsuke of the
Kyoto School.
$1,890 £840

Japanese ivory net-
suke of a tiger preen-
ing its tail, signed.
$2,250 £1,000

18th century net-
suke of a family
of hares by Tame-
taka. $2,250 £1,000

Japanese ivory net-
suke of a puppy
pulling a string,
signed.
    $2,250 £1,000

Osako School wood
netsuke of a group
of mice.
    $2,185 £1,280

Ivory netsuke by
Masanao the 1st
of Kyoto, damaged.
    $3,375 £1,500

Mid 19th century
ivory netsuke, sig-
ned Mitsusada.
    $3,375 £1,500

Superb horse and
foal netsuke by
Rantei.
    $4,500 £2,000

Carved wood net-
suke in the form
of a Shishi, signed
Tadatoshi.
    $4,400 £2,000

Ivory netsuke of
a tiger, attributed
to Tomotada.
    $4,500 £2,000

Carved hardwood net-
suke of a coiled dragon
grasping the sacred
jewel, attributed to
Sukenaga.
    $4,730 £2,150

Wood Shishi, an un-
signed Kyoto net-
suke of 18th/19th
century.
    $5,445 £2,475

NETSUKE

Late 18th century
ivory netsuke by
Tomotada.
$5,625 £2,500

19th century Nagoya
netsuke of a chubby
mermaid.
$5,625 £2,500

Ivory netsuke of a
basket of iris, 1920,
by Kyokusai.
$6,750 £3,000

Superb ivory goat
netsuke by
Okatomo.
$11,250 £5,000

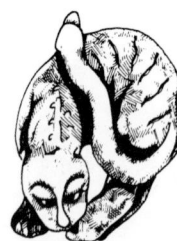

18th century net-
suke of a stylised
tiger by Tomo-
tada.
$12,375 £5,500

Late 18th century
Japanese ivory net-
suke figure of
Shoki.
$16,315 £7,250

Wood netsuke of
an ox by Masanao.
$19,085 £8,675

19th century of
Japanese ivory net-
suke of Kirin and
young by Ikkosai
Toun.
$20,000 £9,000

Finely carved
wooden netsuke
of a Kirin.
$24,090 £10,950

An Oriental pew-
ter circular spice
jar and cover,
7½in. high. $45 £20

Chinese repousse
pewter medical
box, 1850-60,
9in. long. $150 £50

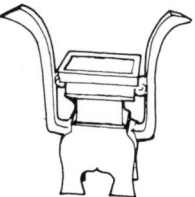

19th century Japan-
ese pewter Ting.
28.5cm. $130 £60

A pair of Japanese pewter pricket
altar candlesticks with pierced stems,
52cm. high. $210 £95

Pair of 20th century Chinese pewter
horse heads, 16in. high. $275 £125

SADDLES

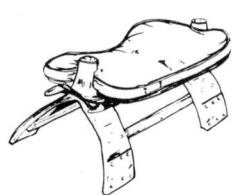

Oriental camel
stool saddle with
a leather cushion.
            $110 £50

Japanese saddle made
in four parts with
holes for lacing to-
gether. $330 £150

An Indo-Persian sad-
dle of mauve velvet
covered with gold
bullion. $1,125 £500

SILVER

19th century
Oriental plated
bowl. $35 £15

Oriental silver card
case with embossed
floral design, 4in.
tall. $65 £30

An Eastern silver
chased and em-
bossed rose bowl,
23cm. diameter,
15oz. $110 £50

Four silver medi-
cine bottles and
another bottle.
    $155 £70

Small 19th century
silver model of an
armed junk.
    $200 £90

Five silver medi-
cine bottles with
matching stoppers.
    $200 £90

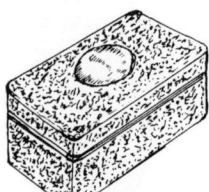

Late 19th century
rectangular box,
4¼in. long.
    $285 £130

Late 19th century
enamelled silver
box and cover,
3in. diameter.
    $475 £215

Chinese silver fruit
bowl, assayed
Glasgow, 1895,
8½in. diameter,
3¾in. high.
    $500 £230

Late 19th century Chinese silver
kettle, stand and burner, 12¾in.
high, 33oz. $530 £240

Late 19th century silver plated
Indian menagerie. $600 £275

19th century
Chinese silver
punch bowl,
84oz. $660 £300

Burmese silver coloured
metal box, circa 1900,
18in. long. $800 £360

Part of an early 20th
century Indian sil-
ver coloured metal
chess set, 37oz.
    $815 £370

One of a pair of 20th
century Persian silver
coloured metal lustres,
17¼in. high, 70oz.
    $815 £370

Crane with silver body
and copper beak, circa
1900, 5¾in. high.
    $825 £375

20th century silver
metal bowl, 11in.
high, 44oz.16dwt.
    $950 £430

SILVER

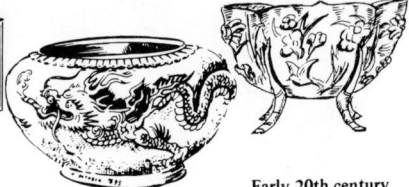

20th century chest of drawers in silver coloured metal, 4½in. high. $945 £420

Japanese Konoike silver bowl, circa 1895, 28cm. diam. $1,015 £450

Early 20th century silver bowl, 9¾in. high, 34oz.12dwt. $1,000 £475

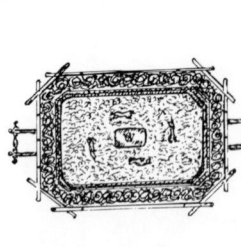

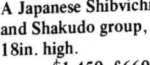

Embossed Indian silver tray, circa 1900, 21in. long, sold with a teaset. $1,200 £550

19th century vase in enamelled silver, signed Tomomitsu, 13½in. high. $1,260 £560

A Japanese Shibvichi and Shakudo group, 18in. high. $1,450 £660

19th century Japanese lacquered wood and silver pair of Kashidako in the form of swimming ducklings on a tray, 19.8cm. long. $1,650 £750

Enamelled silvered metal tray, circa 1900, 11in. wide. $2,150 £1,000

Tang silver gilt scissors, 7½in. long. $20,000 £9,000

104

Chinese silver teaset, circa 1900, 33oz.8dwt. $450 £200

Fine quality 19th century Indian three-piece silver tea service, 43oz.
$475 £215

Indian silver coloured metal teaset, circa 1900, 47oz.16dwt. $550 £250

SILVER TEASETS

Tea service, circa 1900, in silver coloured metal, 60oz.16dwt.
$585 £265

Square sectioned silver Chinese teaset, circa 1900, 62oz.8dwt.
$770 £350

Chinese silver tea and coffee service, circa 1900; 99oz.6dwt.
$1,450 £650

Attractive and unusual Japanese silver tea service. $2,200 £1,000

AGATE

SNUFF BOTTLES

Mottled grey and
russet agate
bottle. $210 £95

Mottled grey and
brown agate bottle
with agate bead
stopper. $220 £100

Miniature grey
agate bottle with
glass stopper.
$220 £100

Mottled yellow
agate bottle with
coral stopper.
$255 £115

Mottled grey agate
bottle with emer-
ald jade stopper.
$255 £115

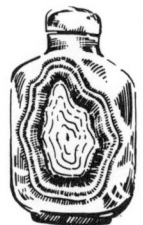

Grey agate bottle
with mottled
emerald and white
jade stopper.
$275 £125

Mottled grey and
brown agate
bottle, with glass
bead stopper.
$340 £155

Grey agate bottle
with red stopper.
$340 £155

A carved agate
snuff bottle de-
picting three
men in a boat.
$340 £155

107

SNUFF BOTTLES
AGATE

A large carved
agate snuff
bottle $375 £170

A fine Chinese
carved agate
snuff bottle.
$1,000 £480

A good Chinese snuff
bottle of grey agate
with brown inclusions,
6.5cm. high.
$4,000 £1,800

AMBER

Amber bottle with
glass bead stopper.
$200 £90

Amber bottle with
green jade stopper
with black collar.
$255 £115

Chinese carved
amber snuff
bottle, 2½in.
high.
$1,600 £725

CLOISONNE

Cloisonne enamel
bottle with match-
ing stopper.
$255 £115

Chinese cloisonne
snuff bottle, of
the Qianlong
period.
$310 £140

Chinese cloisonne
snuff bottle, of
the Qianlong
period. $330 £150

108

19th century Chinese
interior painted snuff
bottle, 6cm. high.
$45 £20

Late 19th century
interior painted
glass snuff bottle.
$55 £25

Red glass
snuff bottle.
$90 £40

19th century
interior painted
snuff bottle.
$145 £65

A 19th century
white glass snuff
bottle with red
overlay.
$155 £70

Mottled white and
russet glass bottle
with carved coral
stopper. $155 £70

Yellow glass bottle
with flattened oval
body. $210 £95

Yellow glass bottle
with tiger's eye
stopper. $220 £100

Interior painted
snuff bottle.
$220 £100

Red overlay glass
bottle with jade
stopper.
$225 £100

Pekin glass snuff
bottle overlaid
with red flowers.
$385 £170

Black overlay glass
bottle with quartz
stopper.
$385 £170

Red overlay glass
bottle, green glass
stopper.
$410 £185

Red overlay glass
bottle with two
ponies, with green
glass stopper.
$410 £185

Red overlay
glass bottle
for snuff.
$450 £200

19th century Chinese
glass snuff bottle,
carved at the shoul-
ders and with a coral
stopper. $460 £210

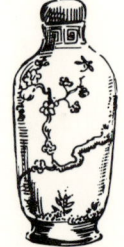

Famille rose Pekin
glass bottle, mott-
led jade stopper.
$475 £215

Early interior
painted Chinese
snuff bottle.
$500 £230

Unusual interior
painted snuff
bottle.
  $575 £260

Interior painted
snuff bottle by
Ten Yu-t'ien,
dated 1907.
     $675 £300

An inside painted
Chinese snuff
bottle depicting
horses. $675 £300

Chinese overlay
snuff bottle.
  $700 £325

Early Chinese
snuff bottle.
  $800 £375

18th century red
overlay snuff
bottle.
     $950 £425

A rare portrait snuff
bottle by Tzu I - tzu,
the reverse side bear-
ing an inscription.
    $3,500 £1,500

An interior painted
glass snuff bottle,
signed T'ing Yu-Keng,
dated 'Winter Month,
1904'.
    $6,750 £3,000

Rare enamelled
glass snuff bottle
by Guyuexuan.
  $13,500 £6,000

SNUFF BOTTLES
HORNBILL

Chinese 18th century
snuff bottle made of
bird beak, 7.5cm.
high. $925 £420

Hornbill snuff
bottle with a
rhodenite stop-
per, circa 1890.
$2,600 £1,200

A carved hornbill
bottle depicting
a maiden among
peony branches.
$2,600 £1,200

IVORY

One of two ivory
bottles with mat-
ching stoppers.
$135 £60

Early 19th century
carved ivory snuff
bottle. $185 £85

One of two ivory
bottles with mat-
ching stoppers.
$360 £160

JADE

Mottled green and
brown jade bottle
with grey jade
stopper. $155 £70

A hollowed jade
snuff bottle.
$200 £90

Mottled white,
brown and green
jade bottle.
$255 £115

112

Mottled grey and russet jade bottle with matching stopper. $275 £125

Mottled white and brown jade bottle. $275 £125

White jade bottle with orange glass stopper. $300 £140

White jade bottle with emerald and white jade stopper. $330 £150

A mutton fat jade bottle carved with figures playing chequers. $330 £150

A deep green jade bottle of rectangular form, 2½in. high. $400 £180

Mottled spinach green jade bottle with inlaid metal stopper. $585 £265

A white jade bottle with russet markings, carved with a boy and a tiger. $2,900 £1,300

Well-hollowed jadeite snuff bottle, the opaque green stone veined with darker striations. $2,900 £1,300

Smoky quartz
bottle with tiger's
eye stopper.
$155 £70

Interior painted rock
crystal snuff bottle
and coral stopper,
2¾in. high. $210 £95

Jasper bottle with
gold stone bead
stopper.
$275 £125

Rose quartz bottle
with matching
stopper. $275 £125

Carnelian agate
bottle with car-
ved agate stopper.
$275 £125

Azurite bottle
with mottled
stopper.
$345 £160

Flattened malachite
bottle with quartz
stopper. $515 £235

Purple amethyst
bottle with green
glass stopper.
$575 £260

Carved chalcedony
snuff bottle with a
russet inclusion.
$575 £260

A blue and red decorated porcelain snuff bottle.
$80 £40

One of two blue and white and underglaze red bottles. $170 £75

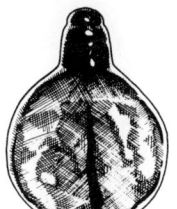

Cylindrical porcelain snuff bottle.
$200 £85

One of three porcelain bottles.
$225 £100

Porcelain bottle with coral bead stopper.
$225 £100

Blanc-de-chine snuff bottle carved with the Immortals, 2¾in. high. $370 £175

Disc shaped opaque white bottle in the Guyuexuan style, 2¼in. high.
$1,300 £600

A Qianlong Pekin enamel snuff bottle painted in famille rose colours.
$3,000 £1,400

A Chinese snuff bottle in Canton enamel with a gilt chased metal stopper, blue Jian mark, 2¼in. high.
$12,000 £5,500

115

One of a pair of soap-
stone Chinese Temple
Dogs of Fo on carved
bases, circa 1860, 7in.
high. $120 £50

Rose quartz group of
two maidens, 6in.
high. $540 £245

Ming dynasty sand-
stone head, 11in.
high. $1,000 £450

10th century black
stone stele, 23in.
high. $1,050 £475

Grey schist stele of
Guanyin, 26in.
high. $1,100 £500

12th century grey
stone frieze, West
Indian, 16½in. high.
          $1,200 £550

11th century red-
stone frieze, 17¼in.
high. $1,200 £550

Rose quartz group
of two maidens,
9½in. high.
          $1,200 £550

11th century buff
sandstone head,
7¼in. high.
          $2,000 £900

11th century Central
Indian Matrika group
in pink sandstone, 33in.
long. $2,500 £1,100

2nd or 3rd century
figure of the Buddha,
17¼in. high.$2,250 £1,000

11th century Raja-
shan sandstone bust
of Bhairavi, 14in.
high.$2,600 £1,200

An 11th century Raja-
shan buff sandstone ram-
pant Simhavyala, 21in.
high. $2,600 £1,200

11th century stone
frieze of the God
Vishnu, 30in. high.
$3,300 £1,500

11th century pink
sandstone figure of
Agni, 33in. high.
$4,500 £2,000

Black conglomerate
marble head from
the Tang dynasty,
9½in. high.
$5,000 £2,250

One of a large pair of
white marble seated
Buddhistic lions, 44in.
high. $5,250 £2,400

Ming dynasty pale
grey granite head
of a Lohan, 10in.
high.$7,000 £3,250

TRAYS

19th century copper circular tray with fluted border. .
$65 £30

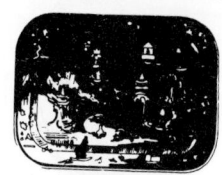

An Oriental brass circular shaped coffee tray, 56cm. diameter, on carved wood stand.
$70 £35

A 19th century papier mache oblong tray painted with a Chinese landscape in gilt, 2ft.6in.
$265 £120

A carved red cinnabar lacquer deep rectangular tray, 11½in. wide. $530 £240

Tomonobu Shibayama letter tray inlaid with mother-of-pearl and ivory, Japanese, circa 1900. $1,295 £575

Japanese lacquer tray with raised border decorated to simulate a tree stump.
$1,500 £700

17th century early Lac Burgaute tray, 13in. diam.
$1,650 £750

A square Japanese lacquer chamfered tray, 16½in. wide.
$1,750 £800

A superb gold lacquer and Shibayama tray signed L. Tsuru-fune, 23¾ x 16½in.
$7,250 £3,300

A Japanese oval silver dagger tsuba, engraved with a simple pattern in kata-kiri. $65 £30

A Japanese iron tsuba showing a chidari perched on a twig, possibly 18th century Goto work. $65 £30

Iron tsuba pierced and chiselled with cherry blossoms picked out in gold. $70 £35

A Japanese iron tsuba, possibly 18th century Mito work. $110 £50

A large iron tsuba, chiselled in low relief with a man bearing a sword Ken, who has frightened an Oni. $140 £60

A Japanese openwork iron tsuba, pierced with stylised bamboo and foliage, signed 'Coshu No Ju Massasaba'. $155 £70

A pierced and chiselled iron tsuba depicting two leaves, the veins picked out in silver wire overlay, signed. $155 £70

Mid 18th century tsuba chiselled in the round with a dragon amidst foliage and waves. $175 £80

Signed and sealed 19th century tsuba, pierced with five rats with golden eyes. $210 £95

A brass tsuba of square form depicting a locust devouring foliage.
$330 £150

Iron Migaki-Ji tsuba, unsigned, Shoami School, 8.2cm. high.
$380 £160

Oval iron tsuba inscribed Soheishi Nyudo Soten Sei, 7.7cm. high. $380 £160

Oval iron tsuba of the Edo period, signed Suihan no shi Shigenaga saku, 8.2cm. high.
$430 £180

Unsigned 18th century oval Shaku-do-Nanako tsuba decorated with flowers, 6.7cm. high. $450 £190

Circular Sentoku Migaki-Ji tsuba, signed with a kao, Nara School, 7.6cm. high.
$525 £220

Late 17th century oval iron tsuba, signed Nishigaki Kampei, 7.5cm. high.
$525 £220

Iron tsuba of Mokko form, 8.4cm., unsigned. $500 £230

Iron tsuba decorated with tangs.
$500 £230

An unusual tsuba of Mokko form depicting dragon flies, chrysanthemums foliage and a fence. $530 £240

19th century unsigned Shakudo Mokko tsuba decorated with a dragon, 8cm. high. $570 £240

Solid silver tsuba carved over both surfaces, 7.2cm. $570 £260

A 19th century Shakudo tsuba of round saucer shape with an old man contemplating a doll resting on his finger. $630 £300

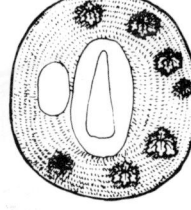

17th century oval Shakudo-Nanako tsuba, unsigned, Hirata School, 6.6cm. high. $810 £340

Rounded-square Sentoku and Shinchu Hariawase tsuba, inscribed Hamano Yasuyuki, 8.2cm. high. $835 £350

A brass tsuba depicting a tiger in relief being pushed by a boy in high relief, signed. $800 £375

Well carved iron tsuba, 8.1cm., signed by Kyokusuiken Okabe Tadamasa. $845 £385

Iron tsuba, 7.7cm., signed Sunagawa Masayoshi. $845 £385

A Shakudo tsuba
of black colour de-
picting three large
silvered dragonflies
in relief, signed.
$860 £400

A pierced brass tsuba
depicting an eagle per-
ched on cherry tree
boughs. $925 £425

A Mito copper and
Shibuichi Hariawase
tsuba. $925 £425

An iron tsuba of squared
form depicting an old
effeminate Sennin, in
high relief of Shakudo.
$1,000 £480

A brass tsuba of Mokko
form depicting many
different types of veget-
ation in relief.
$1,000 £480

Shibuichi tsuba
signed Taizan
Shigeyuki, 7.9cm.
$1,200 £550

Brass tsuba, 6.8cm.,
signed Mensoku Sosei
Taro Sadataka.
$1,200 £550

Shakudo tsuba deco-
rated in relief, silver
and copper inlay,
6.7cm., signed Jury-
usai Yoshinari.
$1,600 £725

Iron tsuba of the
Hiragiya School.
$1,600 £725

Early Edo period
iron tsuba depict-
ing Shoki.
$1,600 £725

Tsuba of Mokko form
by Mikami Yoshihide,
6.4cm. high.
$2,000 £900

Rare copper tsuba
decorated in kata-
kiri with a pair of
Sumo wrestlers.
$2,600 £1,200

Shakudo Nanako
tsuba by Yana-
gawa Naomasa.
$4,250 £2,000

Japanese copper tsuba
depicting Buddha,
Laoste and Confucius,
in finely worked gold
and silver.
$5,250 £2,400

Tsuba formed of
red copper and
sentoku plate,
signed Tshiguro
Masatsune, 9cm.
$5,500 £2,500

Decorative tsuba of
red copper and sento-
ku plate by Ishiguro
Masatsune III.
$5,500 £2,500

19th century Ishigura
School tsuba depict-
ing a cockerel strutting
through some flowers.
$7,500 £3,400

Shibuichi tsuba of
Seiryoken Katsuhira
featuring the three
Sake tasters.
$11,000 £5,000

123

INDEX